Emmanuel Okoloba Coker or better known with his pen name; Eric Coker was born on the 17th of March 1995 in Lagos, Nigeria. He hails from Delta state. He is a graduate of political science and started writing poems when he was in his 2nd year. His first compilation of poems titled "In the name of love and other forbidden topics" was released on the 6th of July 2022 and is currently available on amazon.

Emmanuel adopted the name "Eric" after the passing away of his father, whose name was Olushola Eric Okoloba Coker. He is the last born out of four children. Asides being a poet and an enthusiast for poems, Emmanuel also loves to write short stories with breathtaking cliff hangers which leaves his readers begging for more. His next project following the release of this compilation is due for completion and would be titled "What happened last tuesday" He's currently self publishing and hopes to liaise with a reputable publishing company in regards to his future projects as he hopes to make a career out of his writing.

TO NEW BEGINNINGS...

AND THE MANY POSSIBILITIES THAT COMES WITH IT.

THE "ABOUT" SERIES, WITH OTHER COMPILATION OF POEMS.

ERIC COKER

Author's Note

"To new beginnings and the many possibilities that comes with it" is a project that holds dear to my heart. It's splitted into two parts, and the first part starts with the "About" series where I write about the various stages of where I found myself with life on different occasions and scenarios up till this present moment. I write about my relationships with friends, family and strangers alike, and it also details my experience with personal growth and development and the various means I've gone ahead to either detach or attach myself to entities that's helped to spell out my new growth/strength.

Part two focuses more on my generality with life and the various means and measures at which I've come to learn and experience my reality. I really hope you enjoy the read.

Contents

PART ONE

THE "ABOUT" SERIES

- About Stories and how to rewrite them
- About luck and how to keep on trying
- About being mediocre or mundane
- About being human
- About bad habits and how to unlearn them
- About sadness and getting used to it
- About euphoria and how we get lost in it
- About blurred lines
- About Ex's and heartbreaks (take 1)
- About Ex's and heartbreaks (take 2)
- About Ex's and heartbreaks (take 3)
- About Ex's and heartbreaks (take 4)
- About Nostalgia and how to feel it
- About feelings and how to feel fine
- About boundaries and how to raise them up
- About being lost and found
- About solitude
- About clean slates
- About love and it's many phases
- About home and ways to live in it
- About david and how to dance like him
- About questions you don't want to know the answers to
- About Adam and Eve
- About solitude
- About innocence

PART TWO

GENERAL CONTENT

- The unanimity
- In the name of hope {take 2}
- Mine or Yours
- A small price
- Farce Fable
- Blasphemous Blasphemy
- Significant indifference
- Every woman is a slut
- His lord's prayer
- Nothing but nothingness
- When it rains it pours
- Anthems of a one night stand
- Just friends
- The idea of you
- Arguing is for fools
- Lust; but at what cost
- A thought processed
- The way you make me feel (For Lydia)
- A love Language
- To the girl that wrote me a poem (For Bolu)
- A mind afloat
- Lust; The overflow
- Apologies
- Untitled
- For Jane
- Rinse, lather, repeat
- The bad guy
- Denial

THE "ABOUT" SERIES

About stories and how to rewrite them

And it's in this crazy life I've led,
Pints of blood and sweat; I've bled,
Shades of skin and kin I've shed.
But it was all to what end? After all was done and said.

But let's not pretend, we all vye for a fresh start,
A clean slate, the second part.
I once vied for a heartless heart,
And now I don't shy away from playing the part.
Let's not pretend, we all vye for a fresh start.

The thing about stories is how you write them, my life as a plot; the music man gives it a glorious anthem.
I remain the producer ofcourse.
And a couple of friends and family get some screen time;
Simply because I don't mind them.
The thing about stories is how you plot, produce and rewrite them.

After all is done and said,
This crazy life I've led,
Succumbs to what end?

Ericoker©

About luck and how to keep on trying

I've lost so much, my losses could build a library.
"The library of losses" I'd name it.
I'd stack up my loss in the way that they come, or came, or maybe keep coming. But I'd stack it up nonetheless.

"You see I keep trying my luck"

Ah far down there was when I gave my heart to a blonde. You should read the whole lot. It's a touching one.

A little down right is a compilation of all my returned karma, I'd tell you this, a good deed that goes around takes a long time to come back around. That's what you'd learn if you'd read that lot.

Right by the entrance rests my favourite ones. The kind of loss that built me up. The ones that showed me I had no one. "Have you ever experienced the loss of having no one??" Hmmm. "I think you should read those first."

Ericoker©

About being mediocre or mundane

It's in the mundane.
It's always been.
The brutal simplicity of it all.
If I'm allowed to live, I know I'd let live.
And if I could selflessly give, I know; soon...
it'll be my turn to receive.

But facts can't be deceived.
Lies don't come with receipts,
We live in a world that's cruel and besieged,
With crooked fellows and people steadily taking the piss.

And yet it remains still; in the mundane.
It's always been.
The common simplicity of it all.
If you're allowed to sneeze; and your neighbour says bless you.
If I'm allowed to hold the door as my junior walks before me.
If the weak is given a chance to survive, and the strong lends a helping hand.

If we could all selflessly give, I know; soon...
It'll be our turn to receive.

Ericoker©

About being human

Sure; I fall short of being human
and I suffer the dire consequences.
But who wouldn't?
Who shouldn't?
Who doesn't?

And we all still keep falling only to
pick ourselves back up, and therein
lies our true strength.

Ericoker©

About bad habits and how to unlearn them

And I've indulged myself hard in a lot of vices,
Did drugs, smoked some weed laced with spices,
Got so high I found myself in a spiritual crisis,
Asking myself about my sins?
Asking myself about something.
Asking myself about one thing.
How did "we" get here?.

I know how we did,
It was when you suppressed all your grief,
    Your heart; you didn't know whom it was to give...

So you dashed it out carefreely, you became so easy to hurt, even when you avoided it carefully.

Please learn; It's a bad habit wearing your heart on your sleeve, it's a bad habit suppressing what's meant to be grieved. It's a bad habit giving it all out when some part should be received. It's a bad habit hurting so easily when it shouldn't even be a thing.

How are we going to get there?
I ask myself this one thing.

Ericoker©

About sadness and getting used to it.

And it's never that I relish in my sadness,
Or maybe I do.
Maybe it's just something I've grown to be fond of.

Everything I've known,
Everyone, and places I go,
At some point, all leave.

The anger that I feel,
The hate, the happiness, or the zeal,
At some point, all leave.

But the only thing that stays,
The one thing lurking in the dark that remains,
Is the one thing that I relish in,
The one thing I keep my cherish in.

It's not that I relish in my sadness.
It's just that it's now grown to be a different kind
of pain; a sweet one, the type I keep my cherish in.

Ericoker©

About euphoria and how we get lost in it

And I get lost in euphoria,
Lost in euphoric moments we create,
Mary Jane lays right next to me with a shot of
captain Jack chasing what's left of it.
And we get lost in euphoria.

We lay back in euphoria, unclad; our naked skin
coming together, stained in an unworldly sin.
Still your skin glistens off of your sweat, you seem to
be out of breath till I lick the ebony of your back and
it's like I've listened, to your wants, to what you
want, and your moan suggests to me that you want it
more, and I want some more, and we still get lost in
euphoria.

And you get lost in euphoria,
Lost in euphoric moments we create, when I'm not
sober and you're yet to be hung over. When I was
inside you and the lust took over, the rhythm
calculated, our eyes connected, my limbs pivoted,
your thighs dissected, our eyes connected – our eyes
connected, our lust satiated.

Still we get lost in euphoria.

Ericoker©

About blurred lines

I'm a fine man,
That's got designs for the fine lines;
The fancy side of life.

I don't like the blurred lines,
It's either black or white in my timeline,
Show me what's wrong or right as the times fly,
Don't blur the lines, don't tell me to standby.

I'm a fine man,
You know; the handsome kind.
Tell me what you like and I'd tell you I'm just your type.
Put me on tonight, you are just what the doctor prescribed.

I'm a fine man and you taste like fine wine.
If I put you on tonight, promise you won't return to blur the lines.

Ericoker©

About exes and heartbreaks

An ex once sent me a text about getting back...
Together.

Of course I ignored it.
I ignored her like an ignoramus.
Ignorance is bliss but it gets better when it's done intentionally.

I had an ex who would call me baby,
(She loved me like one too)
She would call me lazy ~ in bed.
She would always go crazy ~ with sex.
I think we had to break up via text,
When our hot sessions became fiery intense.

But how does an 'heart' break?
It starts right after the first ache.

Ericoker©

About exes and heartbreaks (Part 2)

When love left us stranded,
In the middle of the road from where we started...

I was of the opinion, that was the end.
You were with the opinion; we could still remain friends.
You held onto the idea of trying to make amends
Readily ready to follow me through whichever bend.

And I'd swear to my god, that you were perfect.
I remember shooting an aimless shot, till you made yourself the target.
Never coming on too strong; you became the lyrics to my favorite song.

But love, without a second thought, left us stranded...
And now we're in the middle of nowhere,
Not even back to where we started.

Ericoker©

About Ex's and heartbreak (Part 3)

I find myself in a familiar stance yet again.
But I shouldn't be here.
I thought I was prepared.
They tell you "Learn from your mistakes"
But please go easy on me, This is my third take.

Fall in love but please don't get bruised,
Compromise on some bullshit, but don't get used.
I was the fool always in love, I didn't let it be you,
My love language was fluent, yours was hurling abuse.

But after all that's said and done,
Bygones would always remain bygones.
Lol... an ex once told me her love for me would live quite long.
Wasn't surprised either when I read the text a week later that said... "I'm sorry. Goodbye. I'm gone"

Ericoker©

About Exes and heartbreak (part 4)

And I think we should address this,
Before the end begins, before it progresses.

I never wanted to end this,
I'm just so tired of pretending,
Like I'm not in love,
Like I'm only stuck in lust,
Like I lost your trust,
But you lost mine first.

So I think we should address this,
Before the end begins.

I'd tell you what you mean to me,
And you'd casually brush it off like an inappropriate joke, you were never receptive to compliments.
So I learned to keep my emotions in check whenever I'm around you, learned to break the interactions down in steps, slowly climbing it.
But you've built your castle with tall walls and even taller steps and the more I try to reach you there's always the constant need to catch my breath.

And I'm all out of breath.
So I just need to catch myself first.

Ericoker©

About nostalgia and how to feel it

And you should know I miss it;
Those moments when we both could feel it,
I'd text you and you'd text right back,
When I miss your call, I stop, and call right back,
But we seemed to have missed the time track,
An arm and a leg; I'd give to get those times back.

But you should know I miss it;
The way you make it all come easy,
Talking to you, laughing without a care in the world, my loud laughter and your cheeky smile,
Oh gosh, I haven't seen that smile in a long while.
Oh God, I'd have given anything to take away your frown.

And I know I miss it;
And I know love can be stupid;
I know I can be stupid, especially when I feel it,
And you once called me stupid,
Maybe I was the only one who felt it,
But I know I miss it.

Ericoker©

About feelings and how to feel fine

I feel a lot better after I cry,
You'd feel a lot better after I tell you a lie.
And I'd cross my heart and hope to die,
I'd tell you the truth like I'm telling a lie,
That you're not the one,
That there was one before,
That I didn't see your text and call,
When I really just ignored it all.

But I feel a lot better after I cry,
Would we feel a lot better after we die?
Would I feel a lot better, if I gave it a try?
Alas, Everything gets better, in due time.

But for this while, I'd keep crying till I feel fine.

Ericoker©

About boundaries;
and how to raise them up

Without an intent,
I learnt how to be intentional.
Next is to learn how I reclaim my voice,
Explaining to people that this is my choice.

I've always been too eager to please,
And a lot of people would use that and take the piss.
I'm always easily carried away by the wind,
My head is never in a single space, my thoughts are blinded by a million things.

But let me tell you about boundaries and how to raise them up, start to say "No" and watch those who remain ofcourse; start to take note of the various ways your vulnerabilities show and work on them ofcourse; putting yourself first doesn't mean you've put them past ofcourse.

So raise your boundaries up and raise them high ofcourse.
Without an intent,
Be intentional explaining to people that this is your choice, your course!

Ericoker©

About being lost and found

And there are the lucky ones..

"The lucky ones?" I retorted.

"Yeah!" he replied, with a pitch so high you could tell he was so sure of what he was about to speak off.

"You know, the lucky ones," he continued. "The ones who find love at the end of the day, the ones who eventually find happiness" he concluded.

"Hmmm, and what about the others?" I asked as I watched him lit the cigar which had been hanging in-between his lips the whole while.

"The others?"

"Yes, the others" I pressed on. "The ones who are unlucky"

"Well" he started saying amidst a deep puff of the now lit cigar.."You see, the others...they simply find themselves" he said as he exhaled

Ericoker©

About Solitude

And if I choose to self isolate,
Would you choose to isolate with me.

You see, the world has been infected,
And there seems to be no cure for this rot,
What was once blessed has now been cursed,
What was once jest, is now frowned upon.

So I chose to self isolate - run from it all,
Would you choose to isolate with me,
If so, let's run from this world.
If so, let's hide from it all.
For there seems to be no cure...
For all the damn rot in this world.

Ericoker©

About clean slates

I tell you;
we could start again.

Start again,
from being friends.

But you say it depends,
On if truly my love for you
has met its end...

***

I tell you;
why don't I come back again?

After the last fire you ignited
in my heart gets quenched.

Ericoker©

About love and it's many phases

I've known love in different phases,
I've seen love in different stages.

Love as a brother would say;
I want to protect you.

Love as a sister would say;
I want to care for you.

Love as a friend would say;
I want to to be there for you;

And Love as a lover would say;
I want to be the only one for you.

But you see, there's a different kind of love I've grown to know albeit too late.

And it's called self love.

For you see, love as self love would say,
You're not selfish if you put yourself first, or second, or third. I just want to be the only one to protect, care and be there for you. I want to be your trinity.

And that is love, in its rawest phase.

Ericoker©

About Home and ways to live in it

Where do we call home? Maybe it's another world or another plain where the soul goes as it leaves its mortal body, maybe it's a temporary place it goes to before it rejoins a new body, or a vacant space not shared with anybody.

Or maybe it's you. Maybe home is in the way I've found comfort in the sound of your voice and how you've grown to not be a choice I won't be willing to make, regardless of what it takes.

Or maybe it's me. Maybe home is in the exact place I've chosen to stray from, the same place I take these words from, the same place I make these words form.

Maybe home isn't a place. Just a mind state.

Ericoker©

About David and how to dance like him

I moved to the beat, swayed by the rhythm,
There was no festival, no! not for another season.

I moved to the beat, swayed by the rhythm,
There was no party in town, no! none was found.

I moved to the beat, swayed by the rhythm,
With a smile on my face, no! never with a frown.

I moved to the beat, swayed by the rhythm,
I'd dance like David did, dancing with a gold crown.

I slow down the beat, betrayed by my breathing,
There is no festival, no! at least not in this town.

There is no party, Yes! we searched,
And they said none was found.

But with a smile on my face, never with a frown,
I'd move to any beat, swayed by any rhythm,
And I'd dance like david.
David dancing with his gold crown.

Ericoker©

About questions you don't want to know the answers to

I alienate myself from crowds and I make myself scarce. Where's Waldo? Who knows? Who cares?

No one cares, so I try not to stay too long, I try not to stare too long so i break off eye contacts before their eyes turn south. I brake down on my heart when the road goes too fast. But let's not get distracted, let me get back on track.

There are certain questions you really don't want answers to, even when you think you do. Don't be a fool. Ignorance is bliss as I've been taught to think. So I try not to ask questions, I try to weigh in on my options. They'd say make sure you ask, never make assumptions...I don't.

I make presumptions.
Half of the time I'm right, half of the time it's something to write about.

Ericoker©

About Adam and Eve

And if Adam loved Eve,
You'd ask me, what am I prepared to give?
If I stayed would you leave?
If you left would I grieve?

So we keep running around in circles,
You try to open my eye to the truth,
So I take a bite from your apple.
And I see it.
And I see it like Adam saw Eve.

And when Adam saw Eve,
In truth he was asked, what would he give?
Was he prepared to stay if she leaves?
And if she left would he grieve?

Who's Adam?
Who's Eve?
I'm not really sure what I'm prepared to give,
You're not really sure if you're ready to leave.

Ericoker©

About Solitude

I plan to write;
Describing how I feel inside.
But for some reason,
The notepad stays empty.
And I can't have described this feeling,
Any better.

Ericoker©

About Innocence

I crave so hungrily for innocence,
I'm guilty of so many vices and I've paid my fair share. I've paid my dues.

But when I speak of innocence,
I speak of it as if I was a child,
Born new into the world with rose coloured eyes and arms stretched out; as if to embrace that which I was sent to achieve.

I speak of it as a replica of water.
That see through form that assures any intention, the calm nature of its form and its healing capabilities.

I speak of it as a naked body,
Glorifying its scars, unashamed of nobody.
And I starve for this innocence and yearn for the freedom it brings.

Ericoker©

PART 2

The unanimity

It's always better to know oneself,
Lest, others stress over that on your behalf.
You see; when you're known by the world,
You are a lot of things.
A lot of beings, entities, inside just you.

And some would say he likes to sin,
Others would say he's perfect, he's clean,
But why? Why let them decide for you what's hidden underneath that skin?

It's better to know yourself,
Lest you hear someone say,

   - "I know you and it's something you can do"

But in all fairness, I can do all things through the right that strengthens me, and you can too, if only we stretch this out...

Lol...you know me.

Ericoker©

In The Name Of Hope (Take 2)

I hope one day love will remember our names,
Love will remember the feel of our tastes,
The sins and the many forgiveness we chased.

I hope one day, love will say "why don't you try to stay?"
"You're always in a hurry to leave, I want you to stay just one more day"
Love won't remember the feelings I distaste,
Instead, it'll choose to walk along, in a hurry or at whatever pace.

Still I'd say, I hope one day she remembers my face.
I hope one day I get the courage to return back to that place.
That place; filled with love's lingering tastes.

And I hope one day, you forgive me, and these many sins I chased.

Ericoker©

Mine or yours

There are days I sneak off to ronke's place, just to get a taste of her juice.

There's 3 types of juice a woman's known to produce, and ronke knew the kind of juice a man like me could direly use...

Don't get me wrong, you see I've got a girl,
But, her's doesn't taste quite as well,
As ronke's. And I can or can't assure you if or not, I'm underneath a spell.

Anyways, upon getting to ronke's place, of course I was immediately mesmerised by that beautiful face, that seductive shape, I wished in my mind I could have ronke alone to myself for all of the days...

But wait...
Wait ooo...

What is this I see??

Ronke? Why are there already two drunk glasses?
I know your juice is the kind you steadily produce,
But this news, to share not just you but your juice??
Ha ba!!! I'm really not happy with that news.

Ericoker©

A small price

A small price I have to pay for paradise,
Every time I look in my girl's eye,
Every time I look and I spin another web of lies,
Every time I don't spend the night with her,
Every time I come back home only to deny her.

But it's a small price to pay for paradise,
Because when I'm in adama's hand it's a different sigh,
When I'm wrapped in ronke's hug, it's a warming sight,
When it gets to be amina's turn, I get giddy all up inside,
Every time I give love to people I'm not supposed to, I always pay a different price.

And with you tonight,
I'm with you tonight,
It's a different price I'm gonna have to pay, so let's just decide.

Monogamy would have been out of my way, if only it was the smallest price I'd have to pay for that selfish paradise.

Ericoker©

Farce Fable

I woke up one morning just like this; to see angels smoking cigarettes, what a sight!
The devil passively stood by, mumbling on and on about something called regret.

But hey... Jesus christ!
      was lifted up in a space shuttle,
And we both drove around the universe, floating aimlessly in one of those 'SPACE X' space bubbles.

Yet I ask him...
Is there a heaven where we can all settle?
Where we get to rest our souls,
You know; like when dirt in water settles.

So he said to me, you're on my guest list. I mean Jesus.
      I said christ!
And not in a million years would I have ever guessed this.

I can't forget, yet I don't remember,
The exact details to this fabled subject.

                Ericoker©

Blasphemous Blasphemy...

And if I told you I was royalty, I was king.
Would you believe me? Would you believe in me?

Orunmila flings both his dice and right before our eyes we begin to see them both dance...
One sways to the rhythm of a beat no one but it could hear, and the other; the other just spun around in a majestic twirl.

It swung around in a majestic swirl.

And right before it fell,
It seemed like I was the only one who could tell,
It was just like I was right underneath a spell,
Orunmila!! Orunmila!! I beg you; release me now!!
I begin to yell.

If I told you I was royalty, I was a king. Would you believe me?
Would you believe in me for I've been chosen by the gods?

Ericoker©

Significant indifference

"36 years now" he said.

"Wow" I replied. "Do people still stay that long in love??"

"In marriage, yes they do" he replied, "Not so sure about love though" he continued.

"And what's the trick?" I instantly followed up. "I mean there's got to be one, staying 36 years together with someone requires some kind of special magic if not sorcery" I think to myself.

"We both never forget to roll the toothpaste downwards up, that's it. That's the trick" he said.

I got home and poured myself a glass of chardonnay, you know; the good stuff. And I reminisce about significant thoughts and insignificant ones.

The next morning I wake up, and as I set to brush my teeth I remember the words of the old man and I start to roll my toothpaste downwards up. The start of a new ritual.

I've been living alone for 6 years now, Another 30 years with the toothpaste rolled up sure would be another significant indifference in this lonely life of mine.

Still wouldn't hurt to try.

Ericoker©

Every woman is a slut

"Every woman is a slut and all men are fuckboys"
My old man would say.

"And life is the bisexual freak that fucks us all" he'd conclude with...

I never really had mantras or mottos that guided my life path, but those words came so close.

Every woman is a slut but who's not?

And I'd reply him "He without sin should cast the stone first"

And he'd point his fingers at the mirror; at me, and say "there he goes, the fuckest boy of them all"

In this world of sin, learn to sin uniquely.
Yes all men are fuckboys,
Yes all women are sluts,
Yes you're gonna get fucked by life,
But if you do it right you can do it in a way that's gonna be pleasing.

And who doesn't enjoy a good fuck???

Ericoker©

His Lord's prayer.

My cups overfilled and it's spills to the ground,
My blood's over spilled and it sinks to the ground,
And it calls to you, my chi !!!
It calls to you in anger and a frown.

You are bound to keep; hearsay!!!
And I am like a sheep; hearsay!!!
Led astray, left afraid; hearsay!!!
With hungry wolves in green fields; hearsay!!!

And they say you like the feast; hearsay!!!
That comes from days I'm praying on my feet; hearsay!!!
That anthem, I steadily keep on repeat; hearsay!!!
So why now, is my blood on the ground, over spilled?

That's not hearsay.
But I would dare say!!
That I give my prayers, I'm subjugated...
But in your eyes I'm underrated, or maybe this might just be understated.

My chi !!!
I call to you in anger and a frown,
I call to you, with everything that's let me down.
I say to you!!
"I think it's time you stood up from the ground"

                    Ericoker©

Nothing but nothingness

I hate getting back home and I'm met by emptiness.
Like my mistress, she's laid in her house dress,
seated up, waiting for me.
And I step in...

"Oh you're still here" I say as if I expect nothing less.
I never do. She's always here. There's no reason to
expect something else.

"Yes, I am" she replies.

And I ignore her rants, she starts to say something
about how I'd have felt lonely if she was never
around. I almost feel attacked. But she's right. She's
always right.

Still I ignore her rants, so she flings up her hands
and she hits me. "You don't say you need me, but
you miss me" this time I feel attacked.

"Don't say that" I say back.

But I know she's right. She's always right. It's always
nothing but nothingness throughout life's history.

We go there and we go back.
And it's absolutely nothing we take out.
Still I hate getting back home and I'm met by my
would-be mistress; emptiness.

Ericoker©

When it rains, it pours.

I've got all the time but yet I have none,
I fall all the time, and it takes that extra grace to stand up...

And it's all for what?
All for naught?
Nothing.

I want to feel something,
But instead I feel nothing.
I try to feel something,
Instead I tend to see it coming.
The start of a storm, the drizzle before the rain starts falling.

And there are some days I dance in the rain,
Other days, I tend to bask in the pain,
Steadily coping by, hand in hand with Mary Jane.

In some ways, there are some memories I long to relive again,
And on dark days, there are memories I keep far out, locked away.

I really don't know when it's me they'll be coming for, I just pray on days it rains, it never pours; on me.

Ericoker©

Anthems of a one night stand.

You fill my cup up with wine and you sing me a song...
Oh baby girl, why do you look so fine? Or am I just drunk??

You fill my love up, only for just this night.
And by morning time, I know you'd be long gone.

Ericoker©

Just Friends

It's past 3am and we're both laid up, unclad.
I'm expired in your arms and you're renewed in mine, we've both been fucking from time.

I'd plant my flower inside your feminine vase,
and we'd both grow to germinate in sweaty grace,
I'd pump my seeds all over that naughty face,
Then proceed to repeat it all over again.

And you know I don't like to get tempted, till I get lost in your tempest. You can be such a temptress.

It's past 3am and the taste of you still lingers in my mind, the smell of you, the softness of you, the sweetness of you.
And I'm renewed in your arms and you're expired in mine.

We've both been fucking from time.

Ericoker©

The idea of you.

I see love in you and what could be due, if only we gave this love a tiny chance and try to make things work in advance.
But what we seem to have seems to be something of a situation-ship and I sometimes go overboard with my emotions and I start to drown in these feelings till you reach out like a life raft and save me.

And I know I have you, not just the idea of you, or what could be due even when I know with you; I'd want nothing new.

I know I have you, and you know you have me too.

Ericoker©

Arguing is for fools.

I'd once argue about the heavens and the earth,
How is life given? Is it only through birth?
How is life taken? Is it only just by death?
How is a thought processed? What jinx comes first.
The words or the feelings processed?

But arguing is for fools,
And I'd say just do whatever the heck it is you wanna do.
Life is black and white, but it could be grey too.
I've tried to run around, but only just turn in circles

So learn to be a fool only when the time is due,
And never waste time to prove your points,
'Cos that's what real fools do.

Ericoker©

Lust; but at what cost

I think I've lost my prowess to fuck a girl to a crumbling orgasm. Whence she's weak in the knees, she's heaving like she's gotta catch her breath, and I'm swimming in the pool of her feminine sweat.

But lately I'm the one who gets weak in the knees, heaving like I'm about to lose my breath, swimming in a pool of my many unyielding sweats...

Everyone wants to fuck,
Everyone wants to sex,

But this life keeps fucking us all instead.
I think I haven't lost my prowess to fuck anyone to a crumbling orgasm.
I think I just can't bear to pay the cost of lust anymore.

Ericoker©

A thought processed

I begin to ask within; me.
How did you get here?
What did you tell them?
What's your thought process?

And it's gleam, the feeling I harbor,
Safe in my heart's dock, my ticket to be redeemed.
So I reach even further, farther; within.

And I ask myself;
Was it the lack of a father?
Or something close to that figure that made you lose composure in places you never found closure...
Was it the lack of a father figure?
Go figure.

And I only count my years in digits,
Roman numerals, whatever digs it,
What's my thought process?
What will I tell them?
How did I get here?

Ericoker©

The way you make me feel

I am just like a child with a brand new toy,
Filled to the brim with euphoria and a brand new joy,
a brand new slot, for me to try to shoot my shot at happiness...

And I do...
I shoot, but you too, you're the one who gifted the toy,
and you're well too familiar with the cost of this kind of joy, you don't know if you're to open up your slot,
because you search for something deeper than just.

And whenever we try to discuss,
We get lost from issues that matters most,
And just end up talking about other things, like how did your day go.
I always love it when you talk about your day.
How you ignored that man that tried to force an "hey"
I wish; one more time to see you again.
But I know better now that a shot missed is one never to take again.
At least not in the same way.

Ericoker©

A love language

Physical touch, when your lips meets mine,
There's a rush.
Oh wait...
Let me catch my breath,
You look like you're running out of breath...
As I slowly trace my fingers down your dress,
Your lips still meets mine and our eyes connect,
Physical touch, this is how our body connects.

Loud moans and proud groans, I'm in deep and inspired, soon to expire all of my seeds into you, but you want me to finish things through, so i hold on just long enough...

You can't seem to get enough as I show you the glory of my love language; physical touch. I'm down kissing your crotch, professing love to you in ways you've never experienced before...
Let me catch my breath.
You look like you're running out of breath as I slowly trace my fingers out your dress,
Look at how we've made a mess.

Physical touch, this is how my love connects.

Ericoker©

To the girl that wrote me a poem.

On days I start to crave to feel love,
I think about her and what our story could have become,
would she have won? If I'd fallen in love first. You see,
boys like us like to play the bad game, acting like it's not
these girls that taught us, but let me focus.

If I'm being honest, I've thought about us and what
would have become.
If only I had half the time, and you had half the patience,
if only you had ways to crack the cold walls of my heart
'cos I was willingly ready to play the patient. If only you
weren't used to this act and I wasn't used to being
indifferent. If only there's not a new one that struck luck;
with you. If only...

But I'd say this, for the short period our story did
happen, I want to say a big thank you 'Cos even though
the walls of my heart didn't fall through, you showed me
a new way too.

You already probably know who you are.
Oh I almost forgot to tell you, I learnt how to make my
own chicken suya.

Ericoker©

A mind afloat

And I get lost for days,
In my thoughts and my indespicable ways,
I get lost in vices, indulge myself twice, no thrice.
In more despicable ways till I get lost again.

And who's found?
What's found?
It's profound how my thoughts get loud and vivid,
I'm outbound, whenever it gets too much, uneasy.

But I'm still lost for days,
Trapped in my many indespicable ways.

And when they ask, I say "I'm fine"
And when they pass, I wear a fake smile.

Everyday I'm on a new high,
Everyday I wonder if it's the time to say goodbye.
A mind afloat, like water on a boat...

Oh wait, did I say water on a boat?
My mind's still afloat.

Ericoker©

Lust; The overflow

I see the way you look at me,
I see the lust between those eyes,
You feel the moist between your thighs,
I see the way you look at me.

And you see the way I look at you,
My lust, designed as a sight thrown at you.

So let's throw it to the wind,
And let's make this just a fling,
Let my heart remain with me,
And I'd let yours remain within.

We don't have to be friends,
In truth, all things truly end.
But when I drink from your cup,
And you slurp me all up,
When I moan out your name,
And you scream out the same.

It's then we know, again and again,
That in truth this lust won't ever end,
And with a taste of this lust, we really can't
be friends.

                    Ericoker©

Apologies

I wear my heart out on my sleeve,
I've worn my heart out, constantly on repeat,
And I'd tell you, I'm a liar and a cheat,
I do things secretly, my way, discreet.
Who is he deceiving?
Who would even believe him?

They all do.
They all would.
Cos I wear my heart out on my sleeve.
I've worn my heart out, ever constantly on repeat.
And you'd tell me, you're not a liar, definitely not a cheat,
But when I do things secretly, my way, discreet.
You'd see who it is I'm deceiving,
You'd come to terms to believe me.

A truth is the only thing worth believing.
And apologies if wearing my heart on my sleeve
was what made you believe me.

Ericoker©

Untitled

If you're calling to me,
Like I'm calling to you,
Then you should know I've fallen for you,
Like I'm weak in the knees, and you start to whisper these things, softly to my ear, your hands behind my rear, and I still grow weak in the knees.

So you confess your lust to me and moan out sinful words as we both stain this satin sheet, let's not be discreet.

I'd yell out your name, and you yell out his name,
But you shouldn't say it in vain, "oh God".

I'm lost in your lust.
You're lost in these thrusts this missionary pose brings forth. oh Fuck.

Ericoker©

For Jane

So you make wrong assumptions of me,
And I'm never one to prove you wrong,
So I prove you right, I lose this fight.
I lost that fight.
I'm tired of losing, you saw it on my face that night.

So I give it up and raise my white flag,
Mary Jane keeps me up and we pass around the drag...
Mary jane stays the night and we pass around the grass,
Mary Jane lights it up and I pass another class; in self enlightenment.

But you make wrong assumptions of me,
And I'm never one to do you wrong,
Maybe once, I messed it all up,
Maybe once, equates to summing it all up.

You saw it on my face that night.
I'm tired of losing,
So maybe once, I'd give in and give it all up.

Ericoker©

Rinse, lather, repeat.

Love is all he needs.
Love is all she gives.

But Love is never enough...
Oh yes!!!
Indeed.

Ericoker©

The bad guy

Picture Al Pacino in scarface,
I'm a bad guy with a scarred face,
Bad guy with a terrible fate,
I'm a bad guy who leaves no room for escape.

But try it if you must,
What would be the thing you try first?

I say "Try me if you trust -"
In your prowess to dish out a ass whooping,
I'd flip that shit around and your ass would get a lifetime beating.
I'm a bad guy with a scarred face,
Picture me as Al Pacino, the baddest guy in scarface.

Ericoker©

Denial

And if I was in denial;
I'd say " I don't love you"
But I do...
I do.

And if I wasn't in denial,
I'd say "will love ever do?"
'Cos love is never enough,
And I know you've had enough,
Enough of this back and forth.

I'd say I love you, if at all you said it first,
I thirst, for love, for companionship,
For all that surmounts to a great friendship,
With you.

But I'm in denial,
I'd never admit i love you,
Cos if I do,
Then you'd be in denial too,
And say you love me too,
But love will never do,
And that's what breaks us two.

                        Ericoker©

THE END

Appreciation.

To every individual who's gone ahead to buy, rent or share a copy of this compilation, I'd like to express my deepest gratitude for your show of support. In a now-world, where we all constantly search for immediate gratification coupled with an immense selfish human nature, you've managed to help keep my dream alive by getting a copy of this book and that negates the general populism of how self centred our world has grown to become (Atleast to me). My sincere wish for everyone is that all our individual dreams all come to pass in the soonest of times and all we wish for; granted.

I really hope to see you all at the finish line. Keep an eye out for my next project titled "what happened last tuesday". Its gonna be a compilation of very interesting stories with over the top cliffhangers, which is bound to keep your eyes and entire being fixated on each page. Thanks once again and do make sure you share or recommend a copy of all my works to your loved ones and strangers alike. Like my father would say, A good thing becomes even better when it's shared.

Back story from "In the name of love and other forbideen topics

In the name of love and other forbidden topics was my very first compilation of poems, it talks about my various escapades with love, life, myself and also a dark period when I found myself depressed and wanting more than what I was getting at the time.

I made the decision to split the compilation into four different parts with each part owning a topic.

Topic one.

In the name of love: I'd like to think that in some way or form we've all come to experience that phenomenon called love, and whilst some of us have been lucky to taste the sweet side of it, others I'm sure haven't been as lucky. And then there are those who've had the bittersweet experience of it.

I count myself amongst those lot and the various compilations in this topic sheds light on said experiences. My favourite pick amongst this compilation is the topic "YOU" because that spoke about the last time i tried to give my heart out and was met by resistance from the other party. Lol.. Another favourite of mine is the topic "The thing about her". I was head over heels with my then ex and till this moment I still think to myself she was the one who got away. I was ready to marry that girl, but love as we all know it, isn't always enough especially in this world of now.

There are terminologies I used to describe these past girls I've had one or two things with which are the names "Jane" and "Lucy", for the sake of anonymity. Jane or Mary Jane in other instances represents my relationship with drugs at the time, as we all know Mary Jane is an analogy for one of the popular psychedelics called "Weed". I think you can do the maths from there.

Topic two.

Lust: Hmmmm *takes a deep breath* this one ehn... The topic speaks for itself and further explaining this would only take me to a place I don't wanna go to this hot afternoon. So i'm just gonna leave this as it is and say; Do kindly enjoy this topic to its full extent. Or I hope you did if you've gotten a copy already.

Topic three.

Death and all his friends: This is a compilation that focuses more on those times i found myself down and depressed ,questioning reasons why i was here and what would be the benefit if i remained here. This world of now has grown so toxic and evil it takes that extra strength just to pick yourself up on days you're down and or depressed.

This topic speaks about my grief and various ways I expressed or lived/survived said grief. I'm gonna say to everyone finding themselves in that tough spot, down position without finding the strength to get back up, look within, the strength lies in you. You can be your own saviour like I was to myself. Of Course this does not negate the fact that you need trusted family members and friends who can help ease out the entire process, but it all still majorly starts from you.

Topic Four

Me, myself and I: The last topic starts with the poem "I'm weird". I've always known to see myself as different from others, not special, just different, and I've questioned my being so many times, found myself to be the different one in a group of bodies that did not resonate with my persona.

Standing out can be tough especially when you're standing alone most of the time and that got to me the majority of times till i learned to see my difference as a call to me being who i'm meant to be. In a world filled with over 7+ billion people, you really dont want to be like everyone else, hence the need to discover who are and who you hope to be and take decisive actions towards those steps.

All in all, my greatest strength I'd say, rests in my kindness and overused heart that's being so used to being used but wouldn't stop giving. And to some extent, all my past experiences detailed in these poems are things that built me up to this present stage.

I know I have a very long road ahead, and I look forward to it with hopeful eyes and a mind ever ready to learn throughout whatever bend. Thanks for reading my works, and keep an eye out for more books coming pretty soon.

More titles by me (coming soon)

- To the one i call love [poem compilation]
- Conversations with Mr X [poem compilation]
- What happened last tuesday [short stories compilation]
- How to self sabotage and the cost of redemption [novel/autobiography]

www.ingramcontent.com/pod-product-compliance
Lightning Source LLC
Chambersburg PA
CBHW070309220526
45465CB00004B/1817